Odds
DON'T JUST HAPPEN IN A CRAP GAME

JOHN DAMRELL

Odds Don't Just Happen in a Crap Game
Copyright © 2022 by John Damrell

All rights reserved. No part of this publication may be reproduced, distributed, or transmitted in any form or by any means, including photocopying, recording, or other electronic or mechanical methods, without the prior written permission of the author, except in the case of brief quotations embodied in critical reviews and certain other non-commercial uses permitted by copyright law.

Tellwell Talent
www.tellwell.ca

ISBN
978-0-2288-8197-1 (Hardcover)
978-0-2288-8198-8 (Paperback)
978-0-2288-8196-4 (eBook)

Understanding the Odds

*E*ach and every one of us has a story. We are all unique creatures living on a sphere traveling through space and time.

Our paths may vary although many times we arrive at the same destination by a completely different route. The questions one might ask themselves can be deep, and there are always many thoughts to ponder.

How Did I . . .???

Why did I . . .???

Who am I . . .???

These questions and others will and do pop up in our daily thoughts as we travel along on our journey.

I've heard and read different religious scholars referring to our different journeys and paths as something preordained, scripted, or simply God's plan—the way it was meant to be. Perhaps you have encountered a similar belief or have been told this yourself?

I cannot agree or disagree. How do we know for certain what lies beyond if we haven't been there and returned? We have scripture and a template on how to live our best lives and right versus wrong. Doing the right thing, especially in those gray areas where right may not be as clearly defined can be challenging. Most of us have passed by someone begging on the street or a homeless person clearly in need. We might give a few coins to some but pass by others. How do we make the decision on whose coffer we fill?

None of us remember our conception or living months while attached to our mother by an umbilical cord. We have little to no recollection of our early lives. Yet somewhere in the process between conception and birth our brains connect to outside stimuli. As we grow and mature our parents, grandparents, and siblings all become our teachers and models and they are assisted by our genetic makeup.

And what about that inner voice? The voice that tells you not to do something, or possibly guides you to a decision. The voice that says, this person is special, or possibly to be leery of this other person. Think back to the individual panhandling on the street and your response. What is your mental or internal dialogue when you encounter someone in need?

Why does this one person motivate you to help when you've passed by dozens of others doing the same thing or in obvious need. It's that inner voice directing you to assist or help.

I'm not referring to a mental illness when I write about that inner voice. Many of our likes and dislikes, actions and reactions are learned . . .but many are not. Do you simply refer to this as intuition? Do you feel that sometimes the road or path you're on is yours and yours alone . . .

This book is a collection of true stories. Stories from my firsthand knowledge and experience. These stories have caused me to ask myself many times the "how," "what," "where," and "why" questions. How was this possible? What possessed me to do that or to go there? Where did that come from (especially when there is no left field) and why me? To wonder if I am the only one who has experienced these events or if they are shared in some way by us all.

As I look back on my life the picture isn't necessarily clear. Sometimes things happened that were outside of the norm and possibly were swept under the rug and forgotten. Then there were the times that caused me to question, resulting in the realization that we are all far from being alone. Some might call this faith, some a God Kiss, or a special blessing.

Do all of us have special angels that guide, direct, and take care of us until our time here is done?

My belief is these events are far beyond coincidence. Additionally, I believe that you, the reader, have stories that have caused you to reflect on this thought. Maybe a chance meeting, some event, or occurrence has left you feeling the grace of a higher power.

I hope you enjoy what you are about to read. May it also strengthen your faith and beliefs.

We are not alone and there are angels among us.

The Odds of a Home Center Deal

Back in the mid-1980s there was a large home center chain with multiple locations around the southern and eastern regions of Texas. Working in the business of floor covering distribution I wanted the flooring products that I sold in their stores. This would be a big win for my business, especially since they were already selling two of my competitors' lines.

I had tried several times to get a meeting with them. Many letters were written, phone calls were made, but to no avail. I just couldn't get past first base. No one was interested in speaking with me or hearing how I might help them increase their sales, profits, or turns of flooring products. I was basically shut out of these stores, which had their home office in San Antonio, Texas. Since I also lived in San Antonio at the time, this situation was even more irritating because I was unable to sell to a company based in my home city. But things were about to change due to a series of chance events.

Returning from a business trip to the East Coast, I needed to change planes in Houston. I arrived in Houston and discovered my San Antonio connecting flight was canceled. San Antonio is just a short fifty-minute flight from Houston. This was long before the events of 9/11, and at a time when you were required to go to the airline's counter in person to make arrangements when flights were canceled or changed. Tight security didn't exist yet and you could basically roam an airport at your leisure.

Reaching the customer service and ticketing counter I was informed by another airline's attendant that they had open seats on their flight to San Antonio. So, as instructed I prepared to head over to the competing airline's counter to acquire a seat going to San Antonio. I was also told that I would be responsible for paying an additional fifteen dollars for the ticket as their fare was higher than what I had paid to the original airline.

As I was conversing with the ticketing agent regarding the process of changing my ticket I noticed behind me in the line a young woman, possibly in her midtwenties who appeared very distraught.

Wanting to help, I turned to this young lady and told her if she was heading to San Antonio to follow me. As we made our way through the airport, I filled her in on what she had missed in my conversation with the agent. Her distressed look I discovered was due to her not having either a credit card or the fifteen dollars in cash. Yes, these were the days before everyone had a credit card or access to ready cash through an automated bank machine. You had to plan ahead and be prepared in case of an emergency.

I told her not to worry. I had a credit card and would be happy to cover her fifteen-dollar fee. She also lived in San Antonio and was coming home from her college in Florida.

Once we reached the other airline counter, I paid the extra fee for both of our tickets. Since we had about ninety minutes before boarding I asked the young lady if she would like to grab a beer, or something to drink. She agreed and we went to the airport watering hole for a cold one and some conversation. She asked me what I did for a living, and I told her that I sold floor coverings. She told me that her father also sold floor coverings. Since I knew almost everyone selling flooring products in my part of the world, I asked who her father was. His last name wasn't someone I knew personally, yet it was very familiar to me. He was the head of the very home center chain that I had been working so hard to infiltrate for years. Wasn't it ironic that I now found myself having a drink with the daughter of the president of the home center conglomerate that I so desired to do business with?

We finished our drinks and boarded our flight. I gave her my business card with my office address since she was insistent about repaying the fifteen dollars I had spent on her behalf. When we finally arrived in San Antonio, we said our farewells, and headed our separate ways to our homes.

The next day was Thursday and the American Thanksgiving. A day I spent with my family, feeling grateful and enjoying the traditions. I really didn't spend much time thinking about the chance encounter other than to wish it could have been her father that needed the fifteen bucks for airfare. I would have even offered him an eighteen-year-old scotch if he would be so inclined to grant me the chance to make my pitch to him. But that is life sometimes!

On the Monday following Thanksgiving, I arrived at my office around 8:30 a.m. Upon entering the building, I was informed that a certain individual from the coveted home center was trying to reach me. I couldn't believe it and returned the call as quickly as I could get to my phone.

Our conversation was light and jovial. The president of the home center chain wished to thank me for ensuring his daughter got home safely. He mentioned how his daughter should have never been traveling without any money but was thankful that she had run into me.

Thinking to myself this might have been the first time a girl's father actually had said that he was thankful his daughter had run into me made me chuckle, but I accepted his flattery graciously. Unexpectedly, he asked if I might be available to meet him later for lunch. Despite not wanting to seem famished, especially just after the legendary eating holiday had passed, I quickly accepted his offer. I was hopeful yet apprehensive to start counting my lucky stars.

When I reached the company's headquarters later that morning, the receptionist warmly greeted me. It was a very different reception today in comparison to the greeting I had received just months earlier when I had made a cold call to see if I could talk to a department manager.

The receptionist called the president and a few others to tell them I had arrived. I really felt quite special. If nothing else, at least I was going to finally have the opportunity to make my best floor covering sales pitch. Maybe, just maybe, I might get an in with this group and be able to sell them something down the line.

The three men the receptionist called came out to meet me in the waiting room. They asked if I was ready for lunch and if I possibly had some time to walk around a few of their stores after lunch. Simple answer—absolutely! What luck. Fortune had finally smiled upon me.

Our lunch conversation was light. They wanted to get to know me and asked the typical questions. Such as, how long had I been with my employer, did I have kids, and how long had I lived in San Antonio. Sort of like an interview without saying it was one.

After lunch we walked together through two of their main stores; they were pointing out things as I gave them my undivided attention. Finally, I was asked what I would recommend for improving their tile assortment. They also handled vinyl sheet flooring and wondered what I might do to increase sales of that product. It was the opportunity I had been trying so hard to make happen. I couldn't believe the chance I had finally been granted.

Wanting to ensure I made the most of the occasion, I requested some time to prepare a formal proposal and it was agreed that I would come back in three days' time to present my pitch.

My proposal was to add an assortment of the good, better, and best tile choices with twelve patterns available. I also suggested they add to their display an automated sheet goods merchandizer that would hold twenty-one rolls—The Floormaster. It too would have a good, better, best assortment with staggered price points. Something to fit every consumer's wallet. I did my best, now it was in their hands to decide.

It was unanimous . . . there was no hesitation or putting the decision-making process on the back burner. They accepted my entire proposal. Soon I would be setting up my tile and sheet goods program in every one of their stores. It was to be my single biggest purchase order to date and was instrumental in my earning a promotion within the company I represented.

A simple act of kindness to a young lady that just happened to be behind me in line . . .what were the odds?

The Odds of a Hayride

Holiday memories are so very special. Remembering back to the times when you shopped in the stores looking for that perfect gift. Gifts and the gathering of friends and family. The lights, the trees covered in ornaments, some holding personal stories and meanings . . . and our annual Christmas hayride. It was such an important tradition and one that we looked forward to all year.

This event started out as a very small affair, as many functions often do. The first year it was simply a friend who pulled a small flatbed trailer behind his truck with a few small bales of hay on board for people to sit on. It was something to let a few friends with their families enjoy together. What was more festive than traveling through our neighborhood looking at the Christmas lights on houses while we consumed warm cider and hot cocoa on the wagon. Throw in some singing of carols as a group and you had a fun time.

As the years went on the truck and trailer went by the wayside. Our kids were getting bigger, and their friends and families were joining in the festivities. Now I found myself renting a larger flatbed truck that would accommodate about forty people along with the required twelve to fifteen bales of hay to seat them all. We continued to creep slowly through the neighborhood never going much over ten miles per hour, never enough to make your hair blow in the breeze. We sang Christmas tunes, talked, enjoyed the decorations, and laughed together. Most importantly, we made good memories of the times spent together having fun and enjoying the season. After the hayride, the Christmas party was moved inside our house were we took delight in being with each other. Lots of great food, drinks, and as much merriment as one could imagine. It was an event that everyone looked forward to and planned on attending. It became an important tradition to everyone.

One particular Christmas I had reserved a large flatbed truck rental, but I was having difficulty in finding the hay. The feedstore that was close by was completely sold out. I was determined to find some and continued to search as the countdown to the event commenced. Finally, with the deadline quickly approaching I found the required bales about twenty-five miles away. A bit far, but they were an important part of the tradition and the overall experience. I didn't think much about the reasons behind the difficulties in securing the needed bales.

After securing the needed fifteen bales we were all set for another magical evening of Christmas good tidings and cheer. The hayride and party was a huge success, and everyone had a great time together. Another year of great memories and time spent with each other.

The following morning as my wife was bagging up the party trash, I confronted how best to get rid of the hay and return the truck. My dilemma was what to do with all the hay as I didn't really want to drive another fifty miles round trip to return it back to where I had bought it. So, I started to consider my options.

The other feedstore close by wasn't wanting the hay. As I drove down the main thoroughfare through our community I was thinking awfully hard on where I could dump fifteen bales of hay.

Suddenly at a stoplight it occurred to me. How about our community's horse stables. They could probably use the hay. Horses needed to be fed and it would be put to good use. Right?

At the next light I made a left turn and headed to the stables. Actually, they call it an equestrian center, but since I had no equestrians in our family I referred to it as a stable. This was to be my first visit ever to their center.

As I pulled through the gate a young lady approached the truck asking how she could help. I told her about our hayride and that I had fifteen bales of hay that needed a home. She asked me to please wait, and she went into the office. Within a short time an older woman came out and asked me to explain again my predicament with the hay. I retold my whole story, explaining I simply needed a place to dump the hay and that I would really appreciate them taking it.

My request was met with tears trickling down both of the women's cheeks.

"This is a Christmas miracle," cried the older woman. "We have been praying all night for a way to take care of our horses. We are low on funds and most of our boarders are out of town." I could see both ladies were shocked and surprised by my wishing to simply give them the hay.

"This hay," she continued, "it's a gift from God."

I must admit I was tongue-tied. I had simply listened to that little voice inside my head that mentioned the option of the horse stables at the light. Now I was here at the horse center and the hay was going to be used for an incredibly good purpose. I got the hay unloaded and listened to all the accolades coming my way just because I had shown up with the hay.

The crisis of the horse feed situation was adverted, the horse ladies were grateful, and I had no more hay dilemma. The problem was solved! What were the odds that I would think about the horse stables, never knowing how much they desperately needed the help. I had the solution to their problem and now had the benefit of knowing I'd helped someone in need.

I have thought about this occurrence many times over the years, and it always comes to mind at the holidays. That little voice telling me to try the stables. The fact that I drove down to those stables without ever having been there before. And that I was welcomed with more gratitude than I had ever expected really was a humbling experience for me. Especially as it happened during a season that is all about giving, and the discovery that it really is better to give than receive. I was blessed by the experience.

God works in mysterious ways.

The Odds of a Hunter

Back in the late '70s, early '80s I became a hunter. I say this more tongue-in-cheek than what truly occurred. Hunting was an activity that I could participate in with my customers. It was like those who meet with their clients on a golf course. It is an activity to enjoy while talking business. Most of my business contacts hunted, and there was something about that camaraderie out in the wilds that established great relationships.

Many of my associates liked to hunt deer. I was really more of just a quail and dove hunter. First off, I loved seeing the deer out in their environment. Second, I could never see myself cleaning or field dressing a buck or doe. Besides, the birds had nothing to fear. I seemed to be a little off on my aim with a shotgun. In fact, it was a campsite joke as to how many shots were fired by myself, and the small amount of game to show for the firework show I provided. Lots of noise with nothing for dinner.

One of the other hunters, who was a close friend, was also having problems hitting quail while using his 12-gauge shotgun.

It became a huge joke for us all—both of us were horrible shots. And of course, we did nothing to improve our aim.

One evening while we were enjoying the campfire, being outdoors, and some libations under a beautiful star filled Texas sky, we decided to take a jeep ride around the property we used for hunting. We had our choice from the several thousands of acres to drive around and explore. We weren't drunk, but we did have a pleasant buzz.

The two of us had been in the jeep exploring for about thirty minutes when we came upon an empty shotgun shell box laying in the road. Our headlights displayed the box clearly, along with the detail of the drawings of the pheasant, quail, and doves decorating all of its four sides. My buddy got out his gun and blasted the box with his 12-gauge shotgun three times. I followed suit and unloaded my shotgun at the box an additional three times. We commended each other for being deadly accurate on our target practice with that box and its pictures of birds.

The following day we were out driving in the jeep when we came across the box that had served as the target during our impromptu practice. We stopped and picked up the box to examine it closer so we could marvel at our accuracy and congratulate one another on our skills. However, my buddy almost started laughing immediately.

The box was full of holes made by the many shots within the shells. The top had been almost completely blown off. But the funny thing was not one bird picture had been penetrated by any of the shot. There were probably fifty holes in the box and not one shot had even grazed a picture of the birds. What were the odds that our random target practice would still result in the salvation of these representatives of the bird population?

I believe that was my last attempt at hunting. I took it as a sign that I was better suited to simply being the designated camp cook, or bartender. Needless to say, it gave all the guys something to laugh about, and it is still talked about today. My shooting skills became legendary and a favorite campfire tale. What were the odds my skills would become the thing of legends?

The Odds of a School Nurse

When I was first starting my own company, I found myself working a lot from home. It was great spending more time with the kids, and I saw it as a bonus benefit. I would see them before school and often I was able to fix dinner and have special desserts prepared for when they got home. My youngest went to the elementary school located directly behind our house. When I was home he could come for lunch through the back gate, and head back when the bell rang signaling that lunch was over.

We lived in a relatively small commuter community northeast of Houston. It was the perfect place for raising my family.

On this particular day, my son had just finished his lunch when we could hear the school bell ringing. He of course went running out the door. About halfway to the gate, he yelled back a little tidbit of news.

"Dad, the school nurse knows Aunt Patty."

"Wait, wait," I yelled, needing more information than this little bit of trivia. But he was gone quick as a flash back to school.

He was nine years old at the time and had a unique way of viewing the world at large. I always enjoyed his observations.

I found his comment a bit strange and was curious as to what he was referring to. His Aunt Patty lived in California, quite a distance from our home. She had only visited us once and had never stayed overnight with us. I don't think a house with four kids, two dogs, two cats, and a ferret appealed to her. Her loss, right! Never a dull moment in our home.

As I pondered my son's comments, I became more intrigued. After all, our last name, Damrell, was somewhat unusual. I decided to call the school and talk to the nurse. Curiosity killed the cat, and satisfaction brought it back—you know the feeling!

I called the school and asked to speak with the school nurse. I introduced myself to her and shared what my son had said as he bolted through the gate.

The nurse laughed and apologized. She said that she had simply told my son that she used to be best friends with a young lady who had the same last name. I asked what her friend's first name was, and she told me it was Melinda. I felt a shiver down my spine. Could this be my sister's old college roommate from San Francisco? The very one who came home with my sister several times over the course of her short college tenure.

"Mel," I said slowly, as awareness of our connection dawned on me. "It's little Johnny."

Again, what were the odds of her working at the school my son attended! We were both in shock to say the least. She had lost track of Patty some thirty years prior. Mel had gone on in school and had become a nurse. I told her all about my sister, her husband, and their life in California. She also shared with me how they had ended up in our community after she and her husband had done a stint overseas.

It was an incredible coincidence, and the best part was when my sister and Mel were able to connect shortly thereafter. My sister and her husband came to Texas several times to visit after this connection was discovered. It was always great hearing the old stories and sharing in the laughter with both couples. The added bonus was I and my family got to spend more time with my sister and her husband.

It was a gift. A gift of friendship lost and then found. What were the odds that little tidbit from my young son would bring about such joy and fun of being together with friends.

The Odds While in Cozumel

Cozumel has always been a favorite spot for diving. I was introduced to this island off the coast of the Yucatán back in the early '80s. Living on the Texas Gulf Coast made trips to Cozumel fairly inexpensive, and it was a quick flight just under two-hours.

I became acquainted with a great dive operation on my second trip down to the island. The head diver was Rodolpho Solterra, and their boat was the Anita. They offered a variety of trips, I had many friends who used their service, and it provided an opportunity to meet new acquaintances on these excursions. Many times, there would be ten to fifteen of us diving from the Anita. The day would begin around nine o'clock with an hour plus boat ride to our first dive spot. We would all make our deepest dive of the day at the first site. These dives were usually between seventy to eighty feet. Once everyone had finished the dive Rodolpho would anchor the Anita off the beach and fix lunch for everyone. It permitted us with a few hours to relax, catch some rays, eat, swim, and just enjoy the surrounding beauty before the second dive of the day.

Three of us decided to go down together on a dive trip in the mid-1990s. This trip would not include the usual large group of divers and was a little off-season. When we arrived at the Anita on that day, which was docked in the little harbor next to the El Presidente Hotel, we were surprised to be the only ones on the boat. I asked where the other divers were and was told that while there was supposed to be three others on the trip, their plane had been delayed.

Appreciating the extra room, I moved myself up to the front of the wide Bertram to relax before getting to the dive spot. About twenty minutes into our boat ride the boat turned around and headed back to its dock. I questioned what was happening and was informed the people whose plane was delayed had arrived and were waiting at the dock. Oh well, it was just a short delay, so I settled back and enjoyed the ride. Rodolpho picked them up and I heard the chatter from my place at the front of the boat. Everyone now onboard we headed out for the anticipated first deep dive.

After about an hour it was announced it was time to suit up. I headed to the back of the boat and started getting out my gear. I introduced myself to the three people who had joined our adventure late. Two men and a woman. One of the men asked where I was from, and I told him Houston.

"Houston," he remarked. "I was in Houston last month for a golf tournament."

"The Shell Open," I stated. "Do you work for Shell?"

The man laughed with just a bit of frustration and irony before replying, "No, I don't work for Shell. I was in the tournament."

Now feeling more than a little embarrassed I asked, "Sorry, what was your name again?"

"Payne Stewart," he replied.

I just about fell overboard. Payne Stewart was one of my favorite golfers to watch. Standing there in his bathing suit without his typical golf knickers and Tam o'Shanter hat had left me totally baffled. Yes it was him, along with his wife Tracey, and good friend Barry. I marveled at my good fortune of being able to meet this athlete and to spend the day with him.

And what a day we had diving, talking, and just having fun. It was so much fun that we extended the boat charter into the evening for a night dive. After the night dive was completed, Barry took all of us to dinner. What a terrific experience and they were three of the nicest people you could ever meet. What were the odds our planned dive trip would provide us with this experience?

Several months later Payne would lose his life tragically due to a plane malfunction and the resulting crash in South Dakota. It was a devastating loss, and I would never have the pleasure of seeing him play the Shell Open again.

I was so fortunate to cross paths with such a legend and a personal golf hero. It was a memorable and pleasant experience. Out of my many, many dive trips to Cozumel what were the chances I would have this experience? This trip will always remain a wonderful memory for me.

The Odds While Diving in Belize

Back in my thirties and forties I loved to go scuba diving any time I had the chance. Along with a group of friends, I dove all over the Caribbean. On one of our big trips we decided to stay on Lighthouse Reef in Belize.

This is a somewhat remote atoll where a small eight passenger plane drops you off on Saturday and comes back to get you the following Saturday. The lodge consisted of concrete block houses sitting right on the beach. The main house was where the meals were cooked and that was the only place you could get anything to eat or drink, other than whatever you might have brought with you. But it is worth the trip as it is an incredible place to dive.

We arrived midday on Saturday. Like most divers on vacation, we were in a big hurry to get into the water. Everyone checked their gear and did a short shore dive to confirm everything was in working order. We then decided that we would do a night dive out on the reef. The resort boat took several of us out at dusk to a remote part of the reef known as the straights or the horseshoe. We suited up and prepared to do a divers roll off the boat.

Due to the boat's lights some jellyfish had gathered, so the dive master requested all of us leave our dive lights off until we were well below the surface. I rolled off the side and started slowly descending below the surface. It was dark, quite black in the water and all I could see was my dimly lit dive computer, which displayed my depth level. I cleared my ears at twelve feet, again at twenty feet, and by the time my computer showed my depth as thirty-five feet I was stabilized for the dive. As I approached the forty-five-foot mark, a large object slammed into my scuba tank. What the h_ _ _!!! I turned on my flashlight just in time to see a large dorsal fin swimming behind me. My immediate thought was, *am I what's for dinner!*

However, my panic mode quickly dissipated when I realized it was a large dolphin or porpoise. This beautiful creature came back again to rub up against me as I continued to descend into the abyss. With your dive light on the reef comes alive at night. Lobsters and sea snakes occupy the sandy ocean floor. The reef feeds on the plankton and minerals in the seawater. Along with my newfound friend, "Dolly the Dolphin," I continued taking in the majesty of our underwater world.

I'd had about thirty minutes of bottom time when my computer showed it was time to start my ascent. As I reached the required depth of thirteen feet for my safety stop, I wasn't alone. My dive buddies weren't the only ones around me. So was Dolly. I let everyone else go ahead to get back aboard the dive boat. I was totally loving my experience with this incredible creature and wanted to enjoy it for as long as I could.

When it was my turn to board, Dolly obviously wasn't ready for our visit to end. She got between me and the ladder and kept trying to nudge me back into the water. I didn't find it annoying but found it rather cute, and I wondered if she lived around this area. I was finally able to board the boat and to my surprise Dolly followed us to the dock at the Lighthouse Reef. Everyone was talking about our experience with Dolly, and I was of course the brunt of a few jokes because the dolphin seemed to have taken a particular liking to me.

The next morning, I got up in time for breakfast, coffee, and to prepare for the morning dive. I had thought about Dolly during the night and about my reaction when I initially saw that fin! My life flashing before my eyes type of moment. As I walked past the dock heading for the main house and breakfast I noticed a big splash . . . it was Dolly! I couldn't resist jumping into the water and the two of us again shared a special interaction. She would rub up against me and I would pet her. Once when I put my hand too close to her blowhole, she gently let me know that wasn't acceptable. It was an incredible experience, one that I will remember for life.

Dolly followed along that week on most of our dives. She didn't make it for our dive in the famous Blue Hole, but she was always waiting when we returned to the beach. It was a week-long dolphin encounter with many photo opportunities.

I hated saying goodbye to Dolly when our week ended. What were the odds that something like this would ever happen again. I had made over one hundred dives prior to this trip, and I had never experienced anything before like meeting Dolly.

The owner of the resort told me right before we left that Dolly probably had lost her mate. Somehow and for some reason she gravitated toward me. In many ways it was like a relationship you have with the family dog but not one you would ever expect to form with a water mammal.

I'll never forget my time on Lighthouse Reef and its magical sights. And I'll never forget Dolly. She was one of God's beautiful creatures, and for a very short time showed me a different perspective of the world that we all occupy. What were the odds that she would choose me to befriend and grant me this wonderful experience?

The Odds of a Flight from Canada

My business always required a substantial amount of travel. Looking back, I was gone a lot from the home front, which placed most of the domestic duties on my wife.

My oldest son, who had become my stepson at the age of three was having some difficulties. He had dropped out of college in Colorado, and we had moved him to Tempe, Arizona to live with my daughter, who was attending Arizona State University (ASU). It was our hope that he would continue his education at ASU; however, this never happen. So, when my daughter finally graduated and headed back to Texas for the next stage in her journey, our oldest son came with her.

My daughter decided to move and work in Austin. Our oldest son decided to take up residence in a spare bedroom in our home. He would play video games from the time he woke up until all hours of the night. My wife thought he was depressed and provided most of his demands regarding food and liquor. This behavior went on for months. He would come out of the room for a meal or to call for a pizza delivery. He also began to drink heavily while playing video games.

To say I was unaware of the behavior would be false. The fact was that I was totally consumed in my business and gone so much that I chose to overlook the situation. I did have conversations with my wife about our son's behavior. She didn't agree with me in terms of some of the issues and since he was her biological son I felt she had the right to make the decisions. Family life as one can imagine was less than ideal in our home during this time.

During this period, I had to fly up to Winnipeg, Canada to meet with a customer. It was to be a relatively short trip with just an overnight stay. The plane would fly from Houston to Minneapolis, where I would change planes to finish the journey to Winnipeg.

My planned customer meeting was to be a standard consultation. We reviewed our program and then went out for dinner and a few beers at a local pub.

I was back at my hotel room by 10:30 p.m. and was scheduled to catch the early flight home at seven o'clock the following morning.

I got to the airport on time and checked in for my commuter flight back to Minneapolis. The commuter plane had two seats on each side of the isle and appeared to be full. As I settled into my isle seat a middle-aged lady asked if she could take the seat next to me.

I of course got up so she could enter our row. After exchanging pleasantries, the boarding process continued and soon we were taxiing down the runway. In a matter of minutes, the plane took off and our flight began.

We had only been in the air a matter of minutes when my seatmate next to me spoke.

"You seem to have a very heavy heart this morning."

A bit surprised by the question, I asked her what she meant. I hadn't encountered this question before in all my years of traveling.

"Something seems to be bothering you," she added.

"No. Just probably a little tired from being out with a customer last night," I explained.

The lady persisted. "Are you having issues with one of your children, possibly a son?"

Wow! I couldn't believe she was asking me such a personal question. And how could she possibly know what was going on in my home. But I didn't back away from her question. Instead, I opened up about my stepson and the issues on the home front.

It is a relatively short flight from Winnipeg to Minneapolis and by the time we were landing this lady next to me had heard all about my family's current drama.

"Please, do me a favor," she asked. "I want you to go home today and put your arms around your stepson. Tell him you love him, but that he must make one of the following choices. He can get a job, go back to school, or he needs to move out. You need to do this as currently you are only enabling his inaction."

I was completely blown away to say the least. It wasn't her demeanor or the instructions but rather the way the conversation had unfolded. It was innocent and raw. I felt a connection with this woman, someone who I had just met less than an hour before.

"I want to give you this," she said as she handed me a business card. "Please let me know how things go."

Odds Don't Just Happen in a Crap Game

As the plane touched down I put her card in my shirt pocket. I thanked her for her time and recommendations. We started the unloading process, and I asked her to go in front of me. She explained that her husband was a few rows back, and she would wait for him.

Once I got off the plane, I noticed the gate for my next flight to Houston was right next to my current arrival gate. I thought I would wait to say goodbye and thank her one last time. I watched the passengers disembarking but my newfound friend was not among them. As I realized that everyone had exited off the plane and she wasn't to be seen, I reached in my pocket to look at her card. It was no longer there.

How could this be? I get business cards from people all the time and I have never lost any of them. I got the strangest feeling deep inside of me. What had happened to the lady and her husband? Why hadn't they come off the plane? Where was that business card?

I slowly made my way to the new gate and waited there for a short time. Soon I began my last leg of my journey home, still pondering the strange experience I'd had. What had just happened?

When I got back to Houston and finally made it home, I didn't do what she had instructed me to do. It just didn't seem like the right time to have a heart-to-heart with my stepson.

A few weeks went by, and I had just returned from another business trip. Things hadn't changed at home. He was still playing the video games and drinking Southern Mist whiskey. He came out of his room and asked his mother what she was planning to fix for dinner. She replied it was going to be chicken.

"I don't want chicken," he said. "I want pizza."

My wife responded with the standard *you know the pizza number* and walked out of the room. I couldn't believe what I had witnessed. My conversation with the lady on the plane came roaring back and slapped me right upside the face. It was time to act and to prompt a change in his behavior. For his sake, ours, and the family.

"Hey Buddy," I said in a lower-than-normal tone, trying to be gentle in my approach. "Come here, I want to talk with you for a moment."

He responded and came closer.

"I want you to know that I love you tons," I began. "As far as I'm concerned you can live here forever, but you must do one of the following. Get a job. Go back to school. Or move out."

These were the options. I continued, explaining how I felt like we were enabling him to stay stuck. He needed to see what was happening in the outside world. He needed to grow, to mature, to have friends, maybe even date someone. He seemed to take it all pretty much in stride. He didn't make any promises or commitments. He just listened to me and went on about his business.

Sometime between our conversation and the following day he relayed my message to his mother. It did not go over well. She expressed clearly that I had no right to tell him to move out, which was the last thing I wanted him to do. But as it turned out he did move, and so did my wife of twenty-five plus years.

Did the lady who sat next to me on the plane have any idea this would happen? Was this what was supposed to transpire? Who was the lady that vanished from my life leaving no trace behind? A psychic, an angel . . . I'll never know but I have traveled over two million miles by air and have never experienced anything like I did on that day during my short flight from Winnipeg to Minneapolis. What had been the odds of me encountering her and acting on her advice? What were the odds this wouldn't still have been the result if I hadn't chosen to act? Perhaps my actions simply sped up what would have happened regardless.

This wasn't the end of a harmonious union. I went on to achieve what I aspired to in business. My ex-wife moved out to help her biological daughter raise her four kids, and the stepson finally got a job in Austin.

The Odds of Being My Father

I loved my father and knew he loved me. He married my mother a few years after the Second World War because he wanted a child. I'm not saying that he didn't love my mother, but she had been married previously and had given birth to two children. One of those children, a boy had died in infancy around the age of six months. The other child a girl became my sister who I also adored and love beyond words.

My earliest recollection as a child was probably around the age of two. I remember my father sitting me on his lap and sharing his breakfast with me. I recall waiting for him to come in from work, knowing he would play with me. He was always a fun guy, full of life, pranks, and jokes. I know where my sense of humor comes from along with the ability to laugh at myself. I am my father in so many ways, and I see that in myself. I also have seen that in my son, and in my granddaughter from an early age.

My father was the one I would run to while growing up if I broke a window or had any sort of altercation. He was nonjudgmental. He always made me feel that I was cared for, and that the problems I encountered were just part of developing from a boy into a man. He was the parent who often brought me lunch when I was in elementary school, helped me with homework when I struggled, and gave me encouragement to be the best that I could be in life. He did this in a very calm, unassuming manner. In my opinion, he was an incredibly special and blessed man.

Life for my parents wasn't easy. My father joined the space race back in the late '50s when the US was caught up in who would be first to orbit the planet, and who would be first to the moon and beyond. Different companies held the various contracts to make the dreams into a reality. There was NASA, Aerojet, Corps of Engineers, UTL, and a whole plethora of companies dedicated to the space race. We traveled back and forth across the US. Sometimes we traveled with the same families, like a caravan of nomads. I went to many different schools. We lived in Iowa, Colorado, Mississippi, Alabama, California, Idaho, and in many various cities within each of these states. Besides the friends that I made along the way, I always had my dad. He was a mentor but also a friend, and a confidant who I always trusted.

Toward the end of the '60s my father decided to get out of the space race. There had been cutbacks and too many layoffs for his liking. It was hard to stay afloat and often he would be forced to find additional work doing menial jobs just to support the family. I should mention that my mother contributed to the family income as well. But my father returned to his original field of refrigeration, and in 1969 took a job as a general foreman of utilities on the island of Yap. Yap is in the western Pacific Ocean and is today a part of the Federated States of Micronesia. When he came back to the United States a few years later he joined the team working for Los Angeles County in refrigeration. He retired from the LA County after a wonderful career.

By the time my father retired I was out of college and working in a career of my own. He was immensely proud of me and often bragged about his son. As I mentioned earlier he had a great sense of humor. He loved *The Three Stooges*, *The Little Rascals*, cartoons, and harmless silly pranks. He also had a special knock he used when coming to a door, or sometimes just on a cabinet in the kitchen for the fun of it. His special knock sounded like knock, knock, space—knock, knock, knock, space—knock, knock, knock, knock. I thought of it as his signature knock. It was always humorous to me.

My dad was in his eighties when he passed. He was eighty-two to be exact. He had traveled to see my family for his birthday in January. He said he was feeling great and was in excellent spirits. Two weeks later he was diagnosed with stage 4 colon, liver, lung, and pancreatic cancer. It was a death sentence that would eventually take him from us. The doctors gave him between six to twelve months depending on how well the treatments worked. It was a very sad time for all of us.

I had a trip that March over to Paris, France. I remember going into Notre-Dame, lighting a candle, and saying a prayer. I asked God to not let my father suffer. If it was time to take him to please take him quickly and with as little pain as possible. I returned from my trip to France and went to see him monthly in California. I was living in Texas and had business to take care of in Washington State and North Carolina. I was on the road a lot, and I knew my father understood why I wasn't always by his side during this period.

I had planned to go back out to see him on the Wednesday after Memorial Day in May. I had talked with my mother, and she told me that he really needed some new pajamas, slippers, and underwear. I bought him several pairs of shorts, pajamas, and comfy slippers. My mom had told me just to bring them with me when I came out in a few days. I thought about what she had said but something inside of me told me to FedEx them overnight. It was about eighty dollars to send the package, but I wanted him to get it sooner than later. He received the package and called me. He could barely speak but he thanked me for the gifts. Then he said that he had to go because he was so weak.

He died on Memorial Day. He went to the hospital, and my sister called to tell me at first that he was all right and not to worry. Thirty minutes later he slipped away and was gone.

I was heartbroken. I had wanted to be with him. I wanted to talk to him one last time. I wanted to tell him how much I loved him and what he had always meant to me. But it wasn't to be, and I caught the first flight available from North Carolina to California.

I arrived at my parent's home and hugged my mother. I knew she had been through a lot, and I wanted to be there to support her. Because she was distraught she kept repeating all the scenarios of what could have, should have, or might have happened. She wanted to blame the hospital, the doctors, and was lashing out in her grief.

I was not as compassionate as I should have been and tried to reason with the grief-stricken widow. Finally, enough was enough and I decided to go to bed. My mother wanted me to sleep in their room and she would stay in the guest room. I had just gotten into bed and was starting to drift off to sleep when I felt the knock, knock, knocking at the foot of the bed. I wasn't scared, and I didn't react. I simply knew that my father had come to either say goodbye or to tell me not to argue with my mother.

The following morning, I tried to find an explanation as to what had happened the night before. Could we have experienced a small earthquake, possibly tremors that I had thought were my dad's signature knock. But I knew there was no quake, no tremors, and I hadn't dreamed it. It was clear to me this was the last communication we had together. A special moment with the man who had meant so much to me. I believe he came to say goodbye and to also let me know everything was fine. He was well, and his spirit was on a journey somewhere none of us have been. What were the odds it could have been anything else but his spirit communicating to me one last time? It was a testimony to the strong bond between both of our souls.

The Odds of a Metamorphosis

There comes a time in probably most of our lives when we question our abilities and career choice. It's not necessarily about whether we can do something or learn something new, but as in my case my spirit just wasn't into it any longer. After eighteen years in wholesale flooring distribution, I found myself at a crossroads. I had always enjoyed sales but now that I was in a management position I was being asked to do things that were outside my wheelhouse. I knew it was time to move on. But what was I going to do? I had a better-than-average salary, a family of six including me, and meager savings. I felt my savings were not sufficient for striking out on my own, and I had limited knowledge of how to run my own business.

Still, I knew that something much better lay in store, so I picked a different path from the one I was on. What I didn't think about initially was how rocky that path could be. I resigned from my position in August and stayed on until the end of that year. This allowed my employer to find my replacement and gave me time to write up what I thought was a decent business plan. I started the new year as a true entrepreneur. My own boss, doing it as old blue eyes always sang, "My Way."

Well, my way or my initial plan was a bust, and I found myself trying to find a fit, juggling balls in the air that I couldn't catch. I was questioning myself on every business decision I had to consider. One fact remained; I couldn't give up. I had a family to support. I interviewed with a few different companies. But the compensation offered was much less than my previous salary. I was told by the VP of one company that I should be applying for his job, and that I was basically overqualified for a sales position with their firm.

I did some consulting work, sold some flooring as a freelance agent, and even taught a course on defensive driving at night to keep the money coming in for my family.

One day during this period I felt as if I were almost at the end of my rope. I would have never done anything drastic, but I was feeling distraught and a huge failure. Something inside told me that I needed some fresh air, and chance to really think. I drove over to a golf course that was virtually empty with a few clubs. I didn't carry a golf bag as I entered the course, but I had a few balls and probably three clubs including my putter. As I walked along the course hitting the balls, I prayed. I prayed to God to help me find myself. I prayed for forgiveness even though I didn't feel deserving of being forgiven.

It was while on this walk that something happened to me. It was a new revelation, a revelation that I could do something totally different within the industry that I was so familiar with. Something to get myself out of the hole that I had dug for myself. I left the course feeling refreshed, reenergized, and most importantly optimistic about my future.

Nothing of true value or worth having comes easy. Success on any level takes work and there are many pitfalls that must be overcome. The one thing I knew for certain was I had always been good in sales. I also knew that I needed to go to my audience and not hang back and let them come to me. I decided to form my own company. I wasn't sure yet exactly what we would be selling so I called it IDT

IDT could stand for Incredible Devotional Tours. Possibly I could sell trips to religious places like Israel and the Holy Land. Or I could use IDT as an acronym for consulting or mentoring. But as fate would have it, I attended a flooring show in Dallas about a week later and International Designer Transitions Inc. was born. IDT came about due to my meeting a man who was selling wood moldings.

The next twelve months of my life was a roller-coaster ride. I was going to sell wood moldings to the flooring industry. It was simple: just oak moldings in any color that might be needed. They could be used as transition strips going from a wood floor to carpet or vinyl. The innovation of laminate flooring was just emerging with a product called Pergo. But people needed moldings for their flooring installations. I started having the wood moldings made by a small company in Texas. It was a mom-and-pop operation with one molder.

It was a start to what would become a business bigger than anything I could have imagined. I went from dealing with retailers to manufacturers. The laminate flooring business was exploding onto the flooring scene. I had an uncle who was an inventor. I told him that I had an idea for a track that would hold moldings down without breaking through the cap sheet of the laminate flooring. I sent him my idea of a single prong track along with a piece of metal shaped in a "U." Using tin snips, he cut the U down the middle and turned it around making a T-Track. Being familiar with the patent process he filed for a patent, and I incorporated this into my profile assortment. The new track system was born, and I now had something to show-and-tell to buyers. Not just an ordinary oak molding but a molding system.

I started calling on all the new laminate manufacturers coming in from Europe to the US market. We also had manufacturers in the US that were making laminate countertops and they quickly adjusted to making flooring to meet the demand. It was a boom market. At first it was just the small manufacturers involved in making the product. Then the bigger ones entered the market, and I got a call from an industry contact who was in the process of developing another laminate line. This call meant my life would be changed forever. What were the odds that things would align and provide me with this opportunity of a lifetime.

People came into my life that changed my small business into a multimillion dollar business. While looking at an opportunity in Washington State, I met my new partner. He owned a large paint contracting firm but wanted to do something else besides painting houses. Together we raised close to half a million dollars through private investors yet we only gave up just 15 percent of our company. We maintained 85 percent of the ownership and all controlling interest. With the money raised we acquired a large building and the equipment necessary to mass produce the moldings. The business continued growing. We now had several large Fortune 500 companies as customers. My partner ran the factory, and I was out in the field selling. It was a relationship that was heaven-sent and truly a blessing. Our business continued to grow to over 20 million dollars in sales.

I still asked myself all the time, *why me*. I had little to almost no start-up money, limited knowledge of running my own business especially one of this magnitude, but it all came together. The people that came into my life during this time I feel were placed in my path for a reason. Was it divine intervention? You be the judge. I can only say the day I spent walking on the golf course in prayer gave me a new life. It gave my family a new life. I am forever grateful! What were the odds that taking a walk to get some fresh air and to hit a few balls would result in such a success.

The Odds of a New Direction

Life is amazing! There is a song by Ray Wylie Hubbard called "The Messenger" and one of the last lines of the song states, "I just want to see what's next."

I thought my company IDT was my endgame. We took on a huge project with a European customer for a large home center chain here in the US. The European company had many patents in the US on the laminate flooring they were manufacturing. They asked the team at IDT to develop a specific style of molding, and they would handle the costs for all the legal fees for another design patent. In turn, they would give IDT an exclusive licensing agreement to produce this product.

The product was produced, the patent applied for, and the purchase orders started coming in like a tornado through Oklahoma. This project was so large that we established a separate plant just to be able to keep up with this business. Unfortunately, just a year into the program the CEO of the European group passed away from a terminal disease. The foreign company was sold to a private equity group who had different ideas on how they wanted to move the company forward with the home center project. IDT as a result found itself in a very precarious position.

We had purchase orders that had been produced and shipped. Other purchase orders were in production, and hundreds of thousands of dollars in milled components were collecting dust in our warehouse. We had all these components and no payments for any of it was received. It was a horrible scenario to find ourselves in. Due to the agreement our hands were tied. We had a loan from the bank for new equipment, a new facility, one hundred new employees on the payroll, and a ten-year-old business relationship that was heading south fast. The European group was attempting a stranglehold maneuver. A hostile attempt to take over and acquire IDT. It left us with no other option but to file a lawsuit in Federal Court. The next three years of the due diligence process is a story all its own. Eventually, IDT won the case, but it was too little too late, and IDT was history.

So now what... I still had great relationships with most of my customers and clients. I still owned Damrell Group LLC. It came to me like a swift bat to the head. I could outsource the work to my closest competitors, having them make the product for Damrell Group LLC. And I could return to my core strength of just selling. I could also venture out and look for additional flooring related accessories that could enhance my product assortment. I joined forces with two well established US companies that manufactured moldings. One made the wood moldings, while the other made the laminate and vinyl moldings. Both companies were family owned and of the highest integrity. I was on my way once again.

Now I had to find the additional items to add to my accessory assortment. I had been hearing about the DOMOTEX, a flooring show that had been going on for several years in Shanghai, China. I had spent a considerable amount on legal fees defending IDT in Federal Court. Now, I really needed a home run, something to get me from the basement back to the penthouse. I obtained my visa for visiting China and off I went to Shanghai.

The Shanghai show was huge. People from all over the world were showing flooring products in multiple buildings at the fairgrounds. I spent my first day looking at the various installation products for floor covering. There was nothing that jumped out at me. I went back to my hotel late in the afternoon and decided to have a beer in the bar. It was there that I ran into two old acquaintances that I hadn't seen in a while. The three of us talked as we had our drinks. They were aware of my dilemma, and what I had gone through with the closing of IDT. Both men suggested that I look at a specific bamboo flooring manufacturer that they were consulting with at the time. At first, I thought bamboo would be somewhat of a conflict of interest. Would other flooring manufacturers want to buy from me if I was a competitor also selling flooring. But bamboo was a specialty product, and not something the other manufacturers were offering. I thought it might just work if I could get a major manufacturer to offer a bamboo flooring line. I would function as the conduit. The US manufacturer would buy the product directly from the Chinese and I would take a sales commission on every container sold. I finished out the next several days in Shanghai learning as much as I could about bamboo. I was now locked and loaded with another line that I believed had merit.

I returned to the US and called one of my largest accounts, a Fortune 100 company that I had been doing business with for over ten years. I asked for a meeting and headed to Georgia to meet with them. There was an interest, but no guarantees. At least I had a real interest in the program I had put together. Testing would have to be done on the products, and they would need to visit the bamboo plant in China. Additionally, they would want specific items, and a color palate.

The program took over a year to launch. I made ten trips between Houston and China over the next twelve months. But everything came together. Soon the purchase orders started coming in and the containers were being shipped. By the end of year two my large customer had purchased over 750 containers of bamboo flooring. I was back up on the top floor, and what a beautiful view it was.

I would be remiss if I didn't give the credit to my Creator. I was simply the conduit, or catalyst of sorts. I was working hard and listening to those voices that speak to you in the middle of the night. The dreams that tell you what you should or shouldn't do.

But what were the odds of it all coming together in a perfect plan? A chance meeting in a bar. A conversation that led to something bigger than I had ever expected. Some may see it as luck, or the result of just being in the right place at the right time. I see it much differently. I would call it blessings, grace, or favor. Once again I was asking myself, *why me*, and *what's next*. How did it all work out in this way for me to succeed?

The Odds of Grace in Knossos

On a trip to the Greek Islands my wife and I found ourselves exploring the ancient ruins of Knossos, on the island of Crete. This city dated back several thousand years BC. Homer sung of this city in his Odyssey and of the meeting between Zeus and the ruler Minos every nine years. The city was partially destroyed in 1300 BC by an earthquake and fire. The people in this city had a warning system in place so almost everyone avoided death from these natural catastrophes.

The warning system used were clay jars stored in their homes that contained snakes. If the snakes crawled out of the jars and acted strangely such as trying to head for the hills, the people known as the Mycenaeans would know that disaster was looming.

As we walked through this ancient city with the many other tourists, I stood in awe of the temple which could be seen from almost any place within the city's walls. There were people from all over the world visiting this site. One lady had with her a small dog on a leash. This was a very unusual sight to see among the ancient ruins. We were surprised that the archaeological society that was still excavating in Knossos would even allow a domestic animal on a leash to visit.

An American lady standing close to my wife commented about the dog. She too was surprised to see a little dog on a long leash running around this ancient city. My wife mentioned that we too had a dog, but we tried to use good judgment when we visited any attraction while on vacation.

The American lady inquired about what type of dog we had. To which my wife replied that we had an Australian Labradoodle. The American lady shared that they too had a dog, a Golden Doodle. Next the size of our dogs was discussed, and it turned out we both had medium-sized dogs.

You're not going to believe this, but it turned out both of our dogs were called Riley. What were the odds we would travel all that way to meet someone who had a similar sized dog to ours, a similar breed and had called theirs the same name as ours!

As the two women continued to talk, the American woman's husband approached. He had been across from us examining the way the blocks in the ruin had been laid and reading the explanation signage posted about the area. I commented to him how incredible it was to see this city. He was somewhat of a scholar and was knowledgeable about this period in history. I found him to be very interesting. As we talked, we disclosed more and more information about ourselves. Like peeling an onion, we talked about our careers, family, where we were from, and other little bits of information that naturally surfaced. He had been a fighter pilot and had flown planes for many years. He had retired from the military and worked in Dubai for a period of time. He was a man of many interests and very articulate.

I don't recall exactly how the next subject came up. Possibly it was when we were speaking about the Knossos society, but he said something to me that really struck a chord in my brain. The people and their ruler had survived the great earthquake and fire.

"It was through the Grace of God," he said.

I agreed with him and made a comment about the Mycenaeans obviously being in favor and grace to have escaped this disaster. He then shared with me this treasure that I wrote down and want to pass along to you.

It is letters, representing words that describe the behaviors of graceful people. He added that people who possess grace treat people they encounter on their life's journey in a particular way:

Generosity

Reconciliation

Acceptance

Compassion

Encouragement

G.R.A.C.E.—I was enthralled by what I heard. He continued to explain that his interpretation is that the originator may have meant that if we live graceful lives, we will be generous, forgiving so we can be reconciled, accepting, and have compassion for all persons. Additionally, these individuals will encourage others to have hope and believe in the greater good. GRACE. It's like a guidepost or road map for how to love our neighbor as ourselves.

When we finished speaking my spirit or my inner self felt refreshed and rejuvenated. This was just another man and his wife taking in the sights of Knossos on Crete. But my path had somehow merged with his on this journey. I find it more than a coincidental experience. What were the odds that we would connect on that day, and he would share with me such an impactful thought that made me think so deeply?

What are the Odds

In this book I have shared some of my life stories about what the odds were that I would have those experiences. I have felt a connection for many years now to something much bigger than myself. Our universe is infinite. We are all riding on this small ball as it travels around our sun in our galaxy. Our planet is in the perfect zone, the perfect distance from our star for that spark of life to begin. What are the odds that the pieces would align all together in the correct sequence for this to happen and for us to exist? What are the odds that circumstances come together to provide us with opportunities in life?

We all have stories to tell. Reading these stories I believe provides faith. Hearing the stories of others can help us grow, learn, and get through tough times. I believe we are never alone. Listen, be aware, and be receptive.

As I said, these are some of my stories. I know all of you have stories to tell as well. If you would like to share them with me, I perhaps might put them into another book. My email for you to contact me and share your stories is johnwd10@gmail.com.

May God bless you, and may peace be with you always.